BARBARA SHOOK HAZEN lives in New York City where she is a member of the New York Drama League. She has written a number of books for children, including *World, World, What Can I Do?* published by Abingdon. She holds degrees from both Smith College and Columbia University.

The Me I See originated from Ms. Hazen's childhood desires. "I guess as a child I always wanted to look different than I did, to have curly hair like my brother, red hair like my cousin, long eyelashes like anybody who had them," she says. "I feel so strongly that joy and contentment come from accepting oneself—all kinds of selves."

The Me I See

Barbara Shook Hazen

Illustrated by Ati Forberg

Abingdon / Nashville

THE ME I SEE

Library of Congress Cataloging in Publication Data

Hazen, Barbara Shook.
  The me I see.

  SUMMARY: Rhymed text and photographs enumerate
the physical features that make a person unique.
    1. Individuality—Juvenile literature.
2. Self-perception—Juvenile literature.
[1. Individuality. 2. Self-perception]
I. Forberg, Ati. II. Title.
BF697.H38   155.2   77-10162

ISBN 0-687-23910-9

My best
to all the many friendly me's I see in Otis

I look in the mirror.
What do I see?

Me!
I see the many
parts of me.

I see two eyes.
My eyes are blue.
What color are your eyes?
Are they blue too?
Or brown? Or green?
Or in between?

I can wink one eye.
Can you?

I see two eyebrows above my eyes.
They go down
when I frown.
They go up
when I am surprised.

They're on the place
that's called my face.
What else do I see
when I look at me?

A forehead,
two cheeks,
and a chin.

A nose to smell a rose
and to breathe air out and in.

Below, I see a mouth
to talk with and to shout.

I see lips to kiss with
and a tongue to taste with.
I see teeth to help me chew
and to show in a row
when I smile at myself
in the mirror or at you.

Above my face, what do I see?
I see the tip-top part of me.
I see my head, on which I wear
the covering that's my hair.

Some hair is black,
some blond, some brown.
My hair is red
and hangs straight down.

I take my comb and brush from the shelf.
I can comb my hair all by myself.

On the sides of my head,
what do I see?
Two ears to hear
the sounds around me,
to hear something falling
or Mother calling.

To hear the loud sound of a train
or the gentle tapping rain
pit-a-pat, pit-a-pat, on the windowpane,
to hear the purr of my cat
or the sharp **CRACK!** when the baseball hits the bat.

When I look in the mirror,
what else do I see?
Two legs to hold up
the rest of me.

My legs are the parts
that take me places
when I walk
or skip
or run in races.

I see two feet
for kicking balls
and building blocks,
for putting on
shoes and socks,
for wearing rubbers in the rain
and galoshes in the snow
when it's cold
and winter winds blow.

I look again. What else do I see?
Two arms on either side of me
for throwing balls
and carrying things,
for slipping into sleeves,
and sometimes just for swinging.

I see two hands
to fold
or to hold
somebody else's
when I'm cold.

Two hands to cover my eyes
when Daddy says, "Don't peek.
Surprise!"

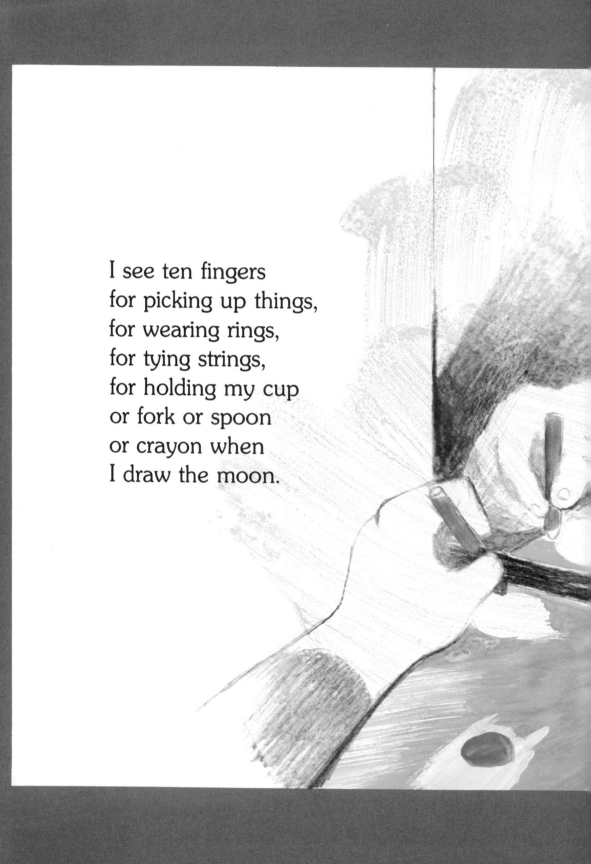

I see ten fingers
for picking up things,
for wearing rings,
for tying strings,
for holding my cup
or fork or spoon
or crayon when
I draw the moon.

I also see the middle of me.
That's the part called my body.
That's the part I put in the tub
every day and scrub, scrub, scrub.

That's the part on which I wear
outer clothes and underwear.

When all of me
is scrubbed and dressed,
who am I?
Can you guess?

I'm all the many parts I see
put together. I am me.
There's nobody like me
'cause nobody else
looks exactly as I do.

I look in the mirror,
what do I see?
One-of-a-kind,
special me.

I'm glad to be
the me I see.

I'm happy too
that you are you.